HAL LEONARD
GUITAR METHOD

GUITAR FOR KIDS SONGBOOK

Strum the Chords Along with 10 Popular Songs

T0088525

To access audio, visit:
www.halleonard.com/mylibrary

Enter Code
4239-8552-1056-8087

ISBN 978-1-4234-8899-6

Visit Hal Leonard Online at
www.halleonard.com

World headquarters, contact:
Hal Leonard
7777 West Bluemound Road
Milwaukee, WI 53213
Email: info@halleonard.com

In Europe, contact:
Hal Leonard Europe Limited
1 Red Place
London, W1K 6PL
Email: info@halleonardeurope.com

In Australia, contact:
Hal Leonard Australia Pty. Ltd.
4 Lentara Court
Cheltenham, Victoria, 3192 Australia
Email: info@halleonard.com.au

PAPERBACK WRITER

TRACK 1

Words and Music by John Lennon
and Paul McCartney

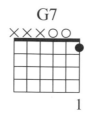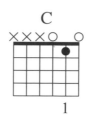

Verse

Dear Sir or Madam, will you read my book? It took me years to write, will you
dirt - y story of a dirt - y man, and his cling - ing wife doesn't

take a look? It's based on a novel by a man named Lear and I
un - der - stand. His son is work - ing for the Daily Mail. It's a

need a job, so I want to be a pa - per - back writ - er,
stead - y job, but he wants to be a pa - per - back writ - er,

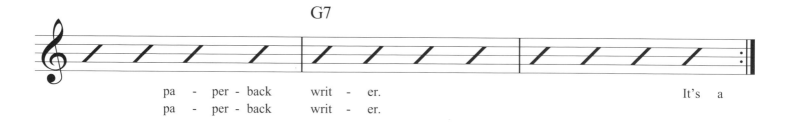

pa - per - back writ - er. It's a
pa - per - back writ - er.

Outro

Pa - per - back writ - er.

TRACK 5

DON'T WORRY, BE HAPPY

Words and Music by
Bobby McFerrin

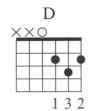 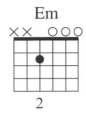 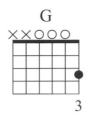

Verse

Here's a lit-tle song I wrote, you
In ev'ry life we have some trouble,

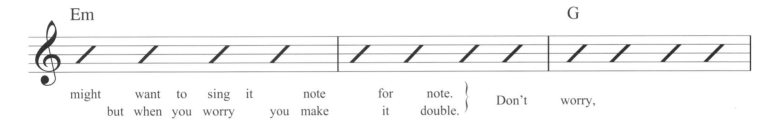

might want to sing it note for note. } Don't worry,
but when you worry you make it double.

be happy.

Chorus

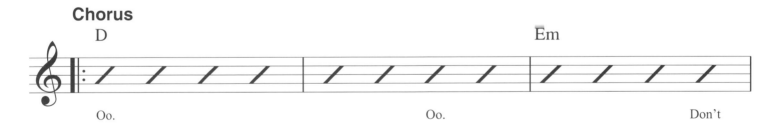

Oo. Oo. Don't

worry. Oo. Be happy. Oo.

Don't worry, be happy.

FEELIN' ALRIGHT

Words and Music by
Dave Mason

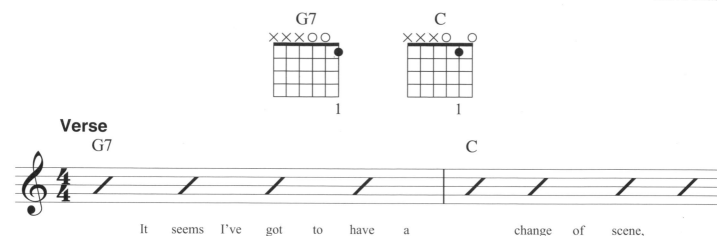

Verse

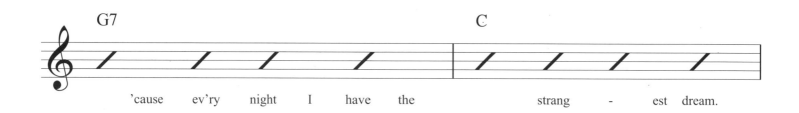

It seems I've got to have a change of scene,

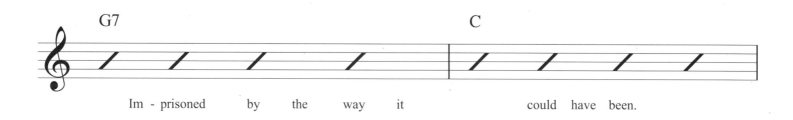

'cause ev'ry night I have the strang - est dream.

Im - prisoned by the way it could have been.

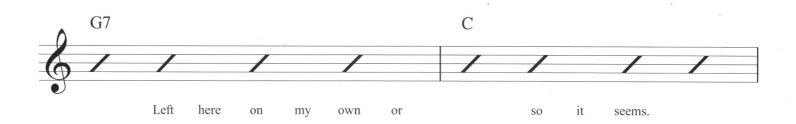

Left here on my own or so it seems.

I've got to leave be - 'fore I start to scream,

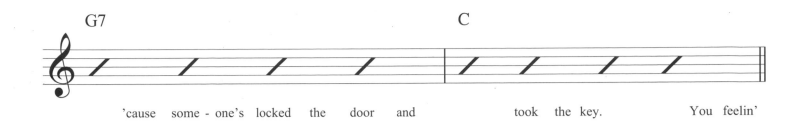

'cause some - one's locked the door and took the key. You feelin'

Chorus

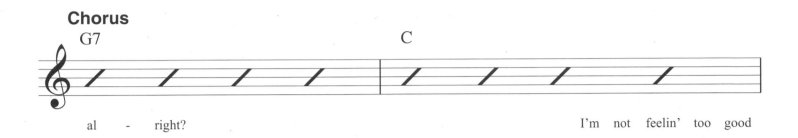

al - right? I'm not feelin' too good

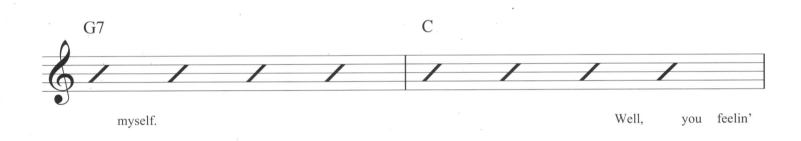

myself. Well, you feelin'

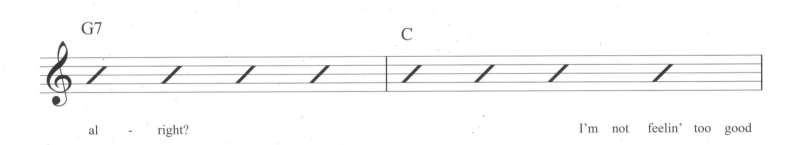

al - right? I'm not feelin' too good

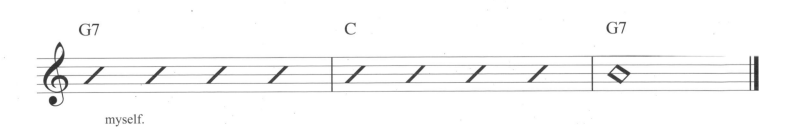

myself.

TRACK 3

JAMBALAYA (ON THE BAYOU)

Words and Music by
Hank Williams

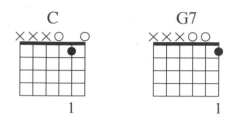

Verse

Good - bye, Joe, me gotta go, me oh

my oh. Me gotta go pole the

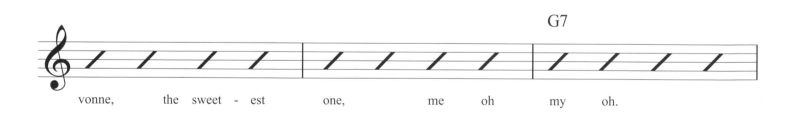

pirogue down the bayou. My Y -

vonne, the sweet - est one, me oh my oh.

Son of a gun, we'll have big fun on the

Chorus

C   C

bayou.   Jam - ba - la - ya and a craw - fish

                    G7

pie   and   fillet   gumbo.   'Cause   to -

                                               C

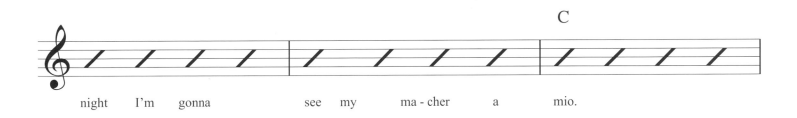

night I'm gonna   see   my   ma - cher   a   mio.

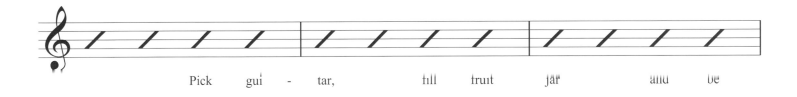

            Pick   gui - tar,   fill   fruit   jar   and   be

G7

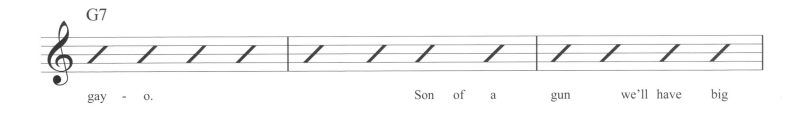

gay - o.   Son   of   a   gun   we'll have   big

                                  C

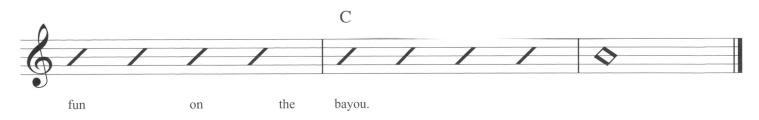

fun   on   the   bayou.

9

ELECTRIC AVENUE

Words and Music by
Eddy Grant

Verse

Now   in   the   street   there   is   violence,   a - na - na

Work - ing   so   hard   like   a   soldier.

lots   of   work   to   be   done.   No place   to   hang   all   our

Can't af - ford   a   thing on T   V.   Deep in my heart I   abhore

washing,   I   na - na   can't   blame   it   all   on   the   sun.

ya.   Can't   get   food   for   the   kid.

Chorus

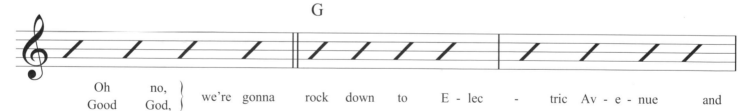

Oh   no, } we're gonna   rock down to E - lec - tric   Av - e - nue   and
Good   God, }

then we'll take it higher.   Oh,   we're gonna   rock   down   to   E - lec -

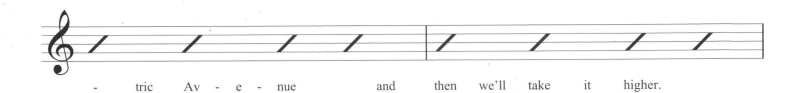

\- tric Av - e - nue   and   then we'll take   it   higher.

1.   **2nd time, skip**   **2.**
          1st ending and
          take 2nd ending   **Bridge**
                                                            G

                              Oh,   no.

Play 3 times

          Oh,   no.   Oh   God,   we're gonna

Chorus
G

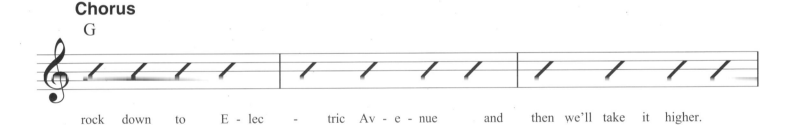

rock down   to   E - lec   -   tric Av - e - nue   and   then we'll take it higher.

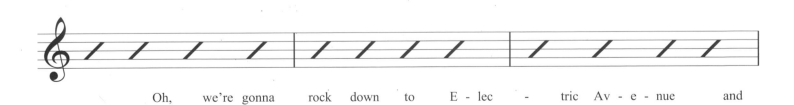

          Oh,   we're gonna   rock down   to   E - lec   -   tric Av - e - nue   and

then   we'll take   it   higher.

LOVE ME DO

Words and Music by John Lennon
and Paul McCartney

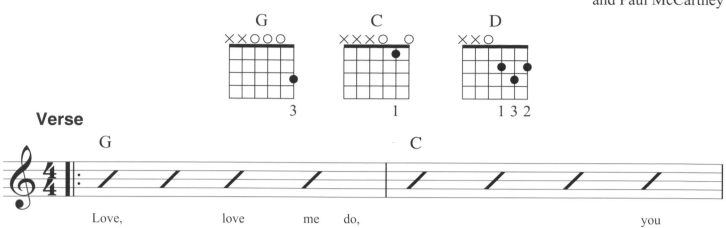

Verse

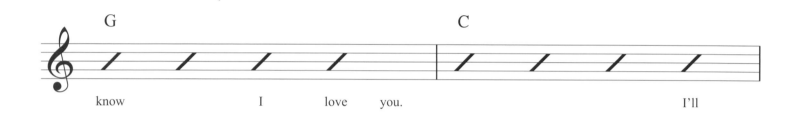

Love,   love   me   do,   you

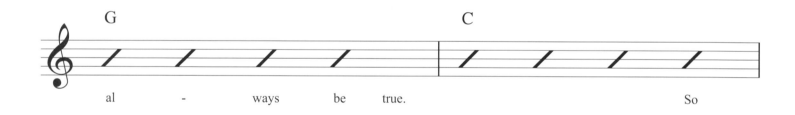

know   I   love   you.   I'll

know   I   love   you.

al -   ways   be   true.   So

please

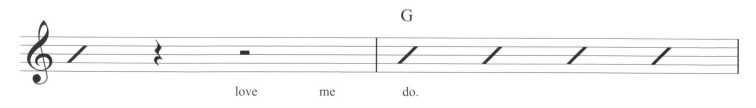

love   me   do.

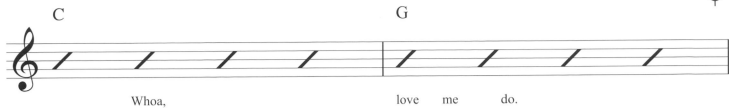

C   G

Whoa,   love me do.

Bridge

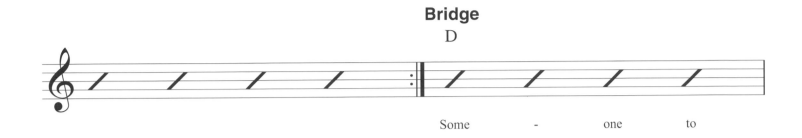

D

Some - one to

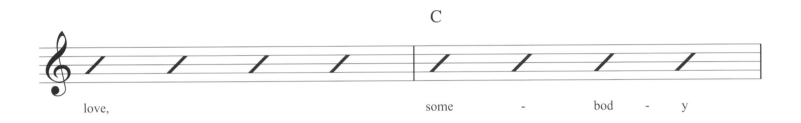

C

love,   some - bod - y

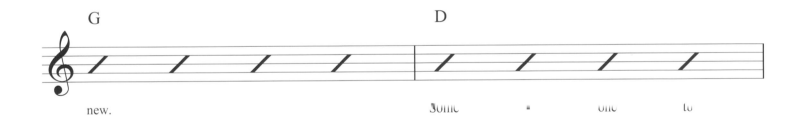

G   D

new.   Some - one to

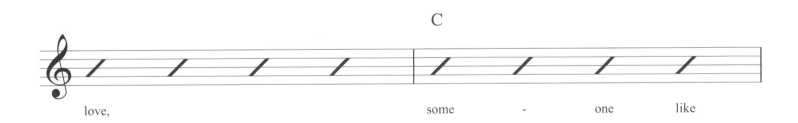

C

love,   some - one like

D.C. al Coda
(Return to beginning
Play to ⊕ and
Skip to Coda)

⊕ **Coda**

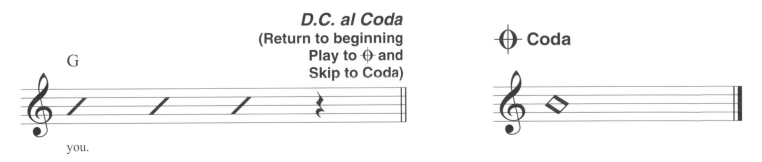

G

you.

13

AT THE HOP

Words and Music by Arthur Singer,
John Madara and David White

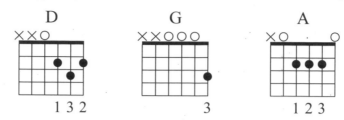

Verse

Well, you can rock it, you can roll it, do the stomp or even stroll it at the

hop.   When the

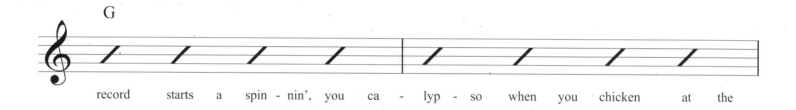

record starts a spin - nin', you ca - lyp - so when you chicken at the

hop.   Do the

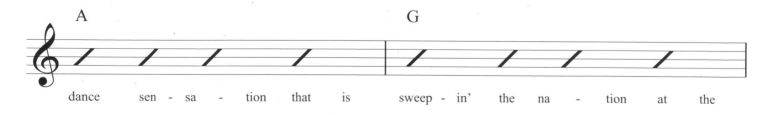

dance sen - sa - tion that is sweep - in' the na - tion at the

D

hop.   Let's go!

Chorus

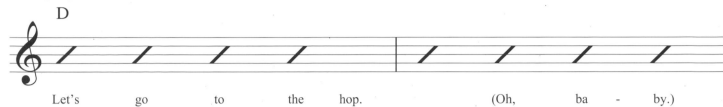

D

Let's go to the hop.   (Oh, ba - by.)

Let's go to the hop.   (Oh, ba - by.)

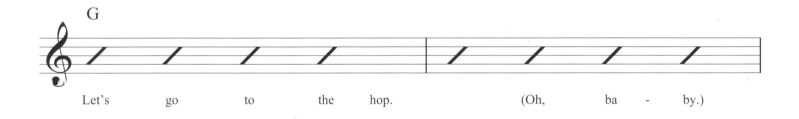

G

Let's go to the hop.   (Oh, ba - by.)

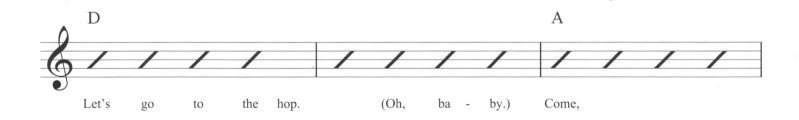

D   A

Let's go to the hop. (Oh, ba - by.) Come,

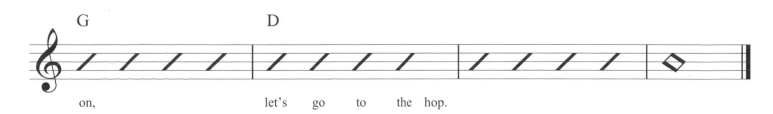

G   D

on,   let's go to the hop.

FLY LIKE AN EAGLE

Words and Music by
Steve Miller

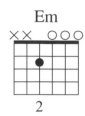 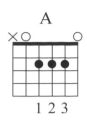 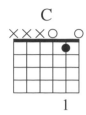

Verse

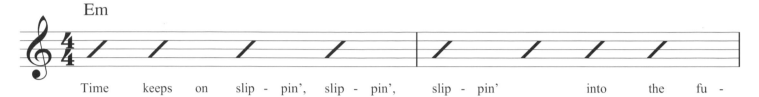

Time keeps on slip - pin', slip - pin', slip - pin' into the fu -

- ture.

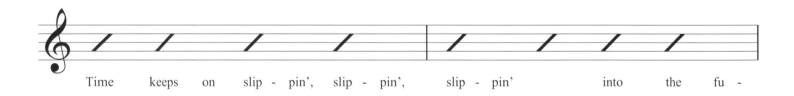

Time keeps on slip - pin', slip - pin', slip - pin' into the fu -

- ture. I wanna

Chorus

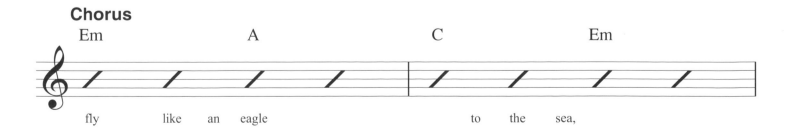

fly like an eagle to the sea,

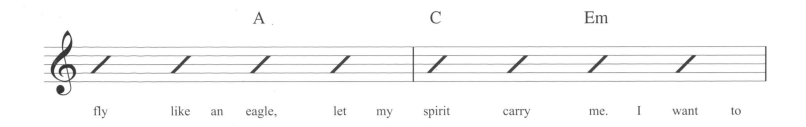

fly   like   an   eagle,   let   my   spirit   carry   me.   I   want   to

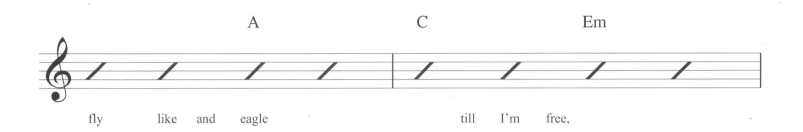

fly   like   and   eagle   till   I'm   free,

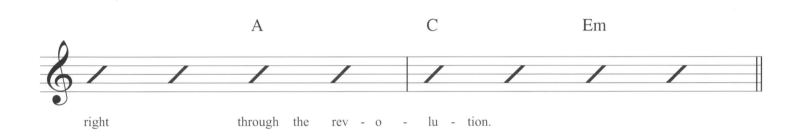

right   through   the   rev - o - lu - tion.

Outro

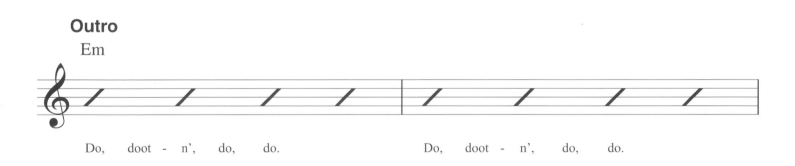

Do,   doot - n',   do,   do.   Do,   doot - n',   do,   do.

Do,   doot - n',   do,   do.

THREE LITTLE BIRDS

Words and Music by
Bob Marley

TRACK 9

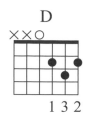 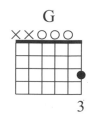 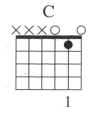 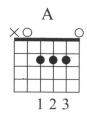

Chorus

D

Don't worry   a - bout a   thing,   'cause

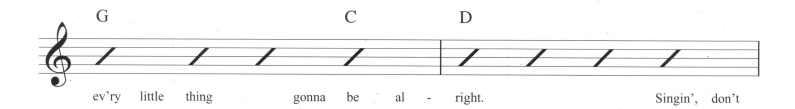

G   C   D

ev'ry little thing   gonna be al - right.   Singin', don't

worry   a - bout a   thing,   'cause

To Coda

G   C   D

ev'ry little thing   gonna be al - right.   Rise up this

Verse

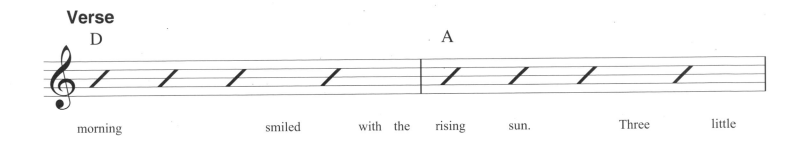

morning   smiled   with   the   rising   sun.   Three   little

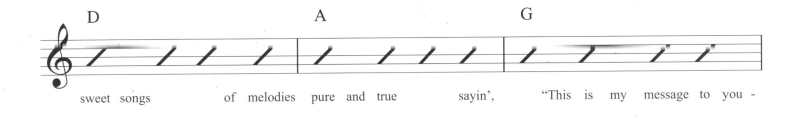

birds   pitch   by   my   doorstep   singin'

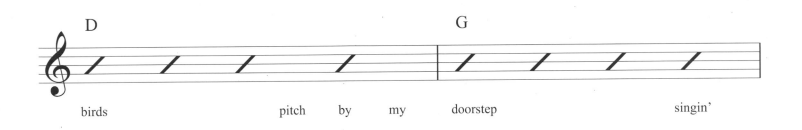

sweet songs   of melodies pure and true   sayin',   "This is my message to you -

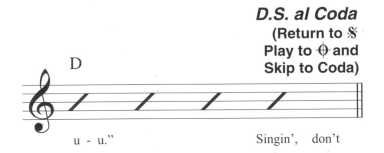

u - u."   Singin',   don't

right.

19

EVERY BREATH YOU TAKE

TRACK 10

Music and Lyrics by Sting

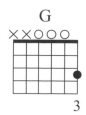 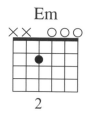 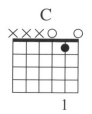 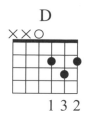 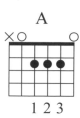

G   Em   C   D   A

Verse

Ev'ry breath you take,   ev'ry move you
day,   ev'ry word you

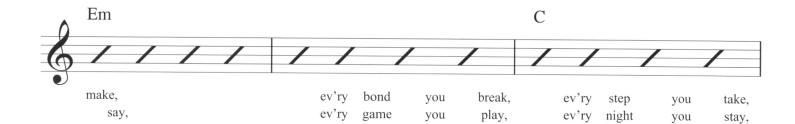

make,   ev'ry bond you break,   ev'ry step you take,
say,   ev'ry game you play,   ev'ry night you stay,

1.   **2nd time, skip 1st ending and take 2nd ending**

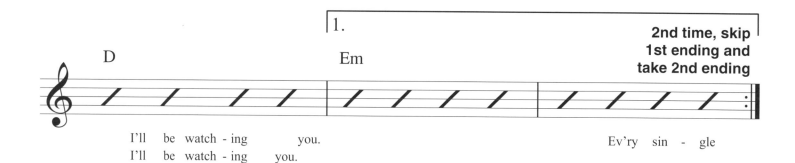

I'll be watch - ing you.   Ev'ry sin - gle
I'll be watch - ing you.

2.   **Bridge**

Oh, can't you see.

you be - long to me.   How my poor heart

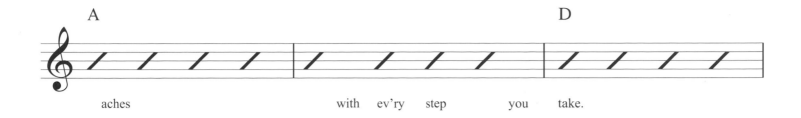

A .... D

aches .... with ev'ry step ...... you ...... take.

Verse

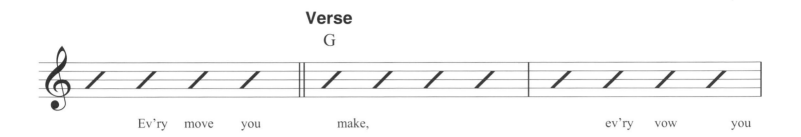

G

Ev'ry move you ...... make, ... ev'ry vow ...... you

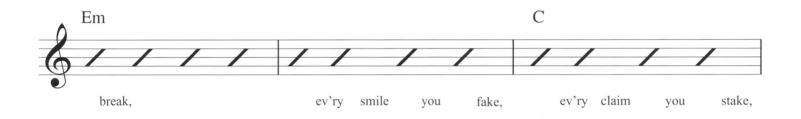

Em C

break, ... ev'ry smile ...... you ...... fake, ... ev'ry claim ...... you ...... stake,

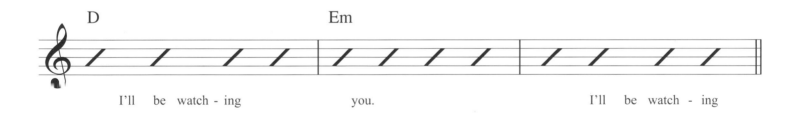

D .... Em

I'll be watch-ing .... you. .... I'll be watch-ing

Outro

G .... Em

you.

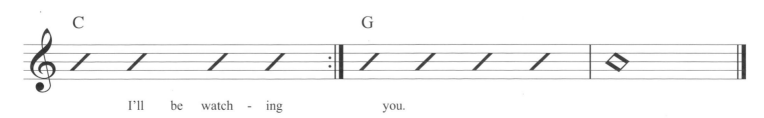

C .... G

I'll be watch-ing .... you.

HAL LEONARD GUITAR METHOD

METHOD BOOKS, SONGBOOKS AND REFERENCE BOOKS

THE HAL LEONARD GUITAR METHOD is designed for anyone just learning to play acoustic or electric guitar. It is based on years of teaching guitar students of all ages, and it also reflects some of the best guitar teaching ideas from around the world. This comprehensive method includes: A learning sequence carefully paced with clear instructions; popular songs which increase the incentive to learn to play; versatility – can be used as self-instruction or with a teacher; audio accompaniments so that students have fun and sound great while practicing.

BOOK 1
00699010	Book Only	$9.99
00699027	Book/Online Audio	$14.99
00697341	Book/Online Audio + DVD	$27.99
00697318	DVD Only	$19.99
00155480	Deluxe Beginner Edition (Book, CD, DVD, Online Audio/ Video & Chord Poster)	$22.99

COMPLETE (BOOKS 1, 2 & 3)
00699040	Book Only	$19.99
00697342	Book/Online Audio	$27.99

BOOK 2
00699020	Book Only	$9.99
00697313	Book/Online Audio	$14.99

BOOK 3
00699030	Book Only	$9.99
00697316	Book/Online Audio	$14.99

Prices, contents and availability subject to change without notice.

STYLISTIC METHODS

ACOUSTIC GUITAR
00697347	Method Book/Online Audio	$19.99
00237969	Songbook/Online Audio	$17.99

BLUEGRASS GUITAR
00697405	Method Book/Online Audio	$19.99

BLUES GUITAR
00697326	Method Book/Online Audio (9" x 12")	$16.99
00697344	Method Book/Online Audio (6" x 9")	$15.99
00697385	Songbook/Online Audio (9" x 12")	$16.99
00248636	Kids Method Book/Online Audio	$14.99

BRAZILIAN GUITAR
00697415	Method Book/Online Audio	$17.99

CHRISTIAN GUITAR
00695947	Method Book/Online Audio	$17.99

CLASSICAL GUITAR
00697376	Method Book/Online Audio	$16.99

COUNTRY GUITAR
00697337	Method Book/Online Audio	$24.99

FINGERSTYLE GUITAR
00697378	Method Book/Online Audio	$22.99
00697432	Songbook/Online Audio	$19.99

FLAMENCO GUITAR
00697363	Method Book/Online Audio	$17.99

FOLK GUITAR
00697414	Method Book/Online Audio	$16.99

JAZZ GUITAR
00695359	Book/Online Audio	$22.99
00697386	Songbook/Online Audio	$16.99

JAZZ-ROCK FUSION
00697387	Book/Online Audio	$24.99

R&B GUITAR
00697356	Book/Online Audio	$19.99
00697433	Songbook/CD Pack	$16.99

ROCK GUITAR
00697319	Book/Online Audio	$19.99
00697383	Songbook/Online Audio	$19.99

ROCKABILLY GUITAR
00697407	Book/Online Audio	$19.99

OTHER METHOD BOOKS

BARITONE GUITAR METHOD
00242055	Book/Online Audio	$12.99

GUITAR FOR KIDS
00865003	Method Book 1/Online Audio	$14.99
00697402	Songbook/Online Audio	$12.99
00128437	Method Book 2/Online Audio	$14.99

MUSIC THEORY FOR GUITARISTS
00695790	Book/Online Audio	$22.99

TENOR GUITAR METHOD
00148330	Book/Online Audio	$14.99

12-STRING GUITAR METHOD
00249528	Book/Online Audio	$22.99

METHOD SUPPLEMENTS

ARPEGGIO FINDER
00697352	6" x 9" Edition	$9.99
00697351	9" x 12" Edition	$10.99

BARRE CHORDS
00697406	Book/Online Audio	$16.99

CHORD, SCALE & ARPEGGIO FINDER
00697410	Book Only	$24.99

GUITAR TECHNIQUES
00697389	Book/Online Audio	$16.99

INCREDIBLE CHORD FINDER
00697200	6" x 9" Edition	$7.99
00697208	9" x 12" Edition	$9.99

INCREDIBLE SCALE FINDER
00695568	6" x 9" Edition	$9.99
00695490	9" x 12" Edition	$9.99

LEAD LICKS
00697345	Book/Online Audio	$12.99

RHYTHM RIFFS
00697346	Book/Online Audio	$14.99

SONGBOOKS

CLASSICAL GUITAR PIECES
00697388	Book/Online Audio	$12.99

EASY POP MELODIES
00697281	Book Only	$7.99
00697440	Book/Online Audio	$16.99

(MORE) EASY POP MELODIES
00697280	Book Only	$7.99
00697269	Book/Online Audio	$16.99

(EVEN MORE) EASY POP MELODIES
00699154	Book Only	$7.99
00697439	Book/Online Audio	$16.99

EASY POP RHYTHMS
00697336	Book Only	$10.99
00697441	Book/Online Audio	$16.99

(MORE) EASY POP RHYTHMS
00697338	Book Only	$9.99
00697322	Book/Online Audio	$16.99

(EVEN MORE) EASY POP RHYTHMS
00697340	Book Only	$9.99
00697323	Book/Online Audio	$16.99

EASY POP CHRISTMAS MELODIES
00697417	Book Only	$12.99
00697416	Book/Online Audio	$16.99

EASY POP CHRISTMAS RHYTHMS
00278177	Book Only	$6.99
00278175	Book/Online Audio	$14.99

EASY SOLO GUITAR PIECES
00110407	Book Only	$12.99

REFERENCE

GUITAR PRACTICE PLANNER
00697401	Book Only	$7.99

GUITAR SETUP & MAINTENANCE
00697427	6" x 9" Edition	$16.99
00697421	9" x 12" Edition	$14.99

For more info, songlists, or to purchase these and more books from your favorite music retailer, go to

halleonard.com

HAL•LEONARD®

EASY GUITAR
WITH NOTES & TAB

This series features simplified arrangements with notes, tab, chord charts, and strum and pick patterns.

MIXED FOLIOS

00702287	Acoustic	$19.99
00702002	Acoustic Rock Hits for Easy Guitar	$15.99
00702166	All-Time Best Guitar Collection	$19.99
00702232	Best Acoustic Songs for Easy Guitar	$16.99
00119835	Best Children's Songs	$16.99
00703055	The Big Book of Nursery Rhymes & Children's Songs	$16.99
00698978	Big Christmas Collection	$19.99
00702394	Bluegrass Songs for Easy Guitar	$15.99
00289632	Bohemian Rhapsody	$19.99
00703387	Celtic Classics	$16.99
00224808	Chart Hits of 2016-2017	$14.99
00267383	Chart Hits of 2017-2018	$14.99
00334293	Chart Hits of 2019-2020	$16.99
00403479	Chart Hits of 2021-2022	$16.99
00702149	Children's Christian Songbook	$9.99
00702028	Christmas Classics	$8.99
00101779	Christmas Guitar	$14.99
00702141	Classic Rock	$8.95
00159642	Classical Melodies	$12.99
00253933	Disney/Pixar's Coco	$16.99
00702203	CMT's 100 Greatest Country Songs	$34.99
00702283	The Contemporary Christian Collection	$16.99

00196954	Contemporary Disney	$19.99
00702239	Country Classics for Easy Guitar	$24.99
00702257	Easy Acoustic Guitar Songs	$17.99
00702041	Favorite Hymns for Easy Guitar	$12.99
00222701	Folk Pop Songs	$17.99
00126894	Frozen	$14.99
00333922	Frozen 2	$14.99
00702286	Glee	$16.99
00702160	The Great American Country Songbook	$19.99
00702148	Great American Gospel for Guitar	$14.99
00702050	Great Classical Themes for Easy Guitar	$9.99
00275088	The Greatest Showman	$17.99
00148030	Halloween Guitar Songs	$14.99
00702273	Irish Songs	$14.99
00192503	Jazz Classics for Easy Guitar	$16.99
00702275	Jazz Favorites for Easy Guitar	$17.99
00702274	Jazz Standards for Easy Guitar	$19.99
00702162	Jumbo Easy Guitar Songbook	$24.99
00232285	La La Land	$16.99
00702258	Legends of Rock	$14.99
00702189	MTV's 100 Greatest Pop Songs	$34.99
00702272	1950s Rock	$16.99
00702271	1960s Rock	$16.99
00702270	1970s Rock	$24.99
00702269	1980s Rock	$16.99

00702268	1990s Rock	$24.99
00369043	Rock Songs for Kids	$14.99
00109725	Once	$14.99
00702187	Selections from O Brother Where Art Thou?	$19.99
00702178	100 Songs for Kids	$16.99
00702515	Pirates of the Caribbean	$17.99
00702125	Praise and Worship for Guitar	$14.99
00287930	Songs from *A Star Is Born, The Greatest Showman, La La Land,* and More Movie Musicals	$16.99
00702285	Southern Rock Hits	$12.99
00156420	Star Wars Music	$16.99
00121535	30 Easy Celtic Guitar Solos	$16.99
00244654	Top Hits of 2017	$14.99
00283786	Top Hits of 2018	$14.99
00302269	Top Hits of 2019	$14.99
00355779	Top Hits of 2020	$14.99
00374083	Top Hits of 2021	$16.99
00702294	Top Worship Hits	$17.99
00702255	VH1's 100 Greatest Hard Rock Songs	$34.99
00702175	VH1's 100 Greatest Songs of Rock and Roll	$34.99
00702253	Wicked	$12.99

ARTIST COLLECTIONS

00702267	AC/DC for Easy Guitar	$16.99
00156221	Adele – 25	$16.99
00396889	Adele – 30	$19.99
00702040	Best of the Allman Brothers	$16.99
00702865	J.S. Bach for Easy Guitar	$15.99
00702169	Best of The Beach Boys	$16.99
00702292	The Beatles — 1	$22.99
00125796	Best of Chuck Berry	$16.99
00702201	The Essential Black Sabbath	$15.99
00702250	blink-182 — Greatest Hits	$17.99
02501615	Zac Brown Band — The Foundation	$17.99
02501621	Zac Brown Band — You Get What You Give	$16.99
00702043	Best of Johnny Cash	$17.99
00702090	Eric Clapton's Best	$16.99
00702086	Eric Clapton — from the Album Unplugged	$17.99
00702202	The Essential Eric Clapton	$17.99
00702053	Best of Patsy Cline	$17.99
00222697	Very Best of Coldplay – 2nd Edition	$17.99
00702229	The Very Best of Creedence Clearwater Revival	$16.99
00702145	Best of Jim Croce	$16.99
00702278	Crosby, Stills & Nash	$12.99
14042809	Bob Dylan	$15.99
00702276	Fleetwood Mac — Easy Guitar Collection	$17.99
00139462	The Very Best of Grateful Dead	$16.99
00702136	Best of Merle Haggard	$16.99
00702227	Jimi Hendrix — Smash Hits	$19.99
00702288	Best of Hillsong United	$12.99
00702236	Best of Antonio Carlos Jobim	$15.99

00702245	Elton John — Greatest Hits 1970–2002	$19.99
00129855	Jack Johnson	$17.99
00702204	Robert Johnson	$16.99
00702234	Selections from Toby Keith — 35 Biggest Hits	$12.95
00702003	Kiss	$16.99
00702216	Lynyrd Skynyrd	$17.99
00702182	The Essential Bob Marley	$16.99
00146081	Maroon 5	$14.99
00121925	Bruno Mars – Unorthodox Jukebox	$12.99
00702248	Paul McCartney — All the Best	$14.99
00125484	The Best of MercyMe	$12.99
00702209	Steve Miller Band — Young Hearts (Greatest Hits)	$12.95
00124167	Jason Mraz	$15.99
00702096	Best of Nirvana	$16.99
00702211	The Offspring — Greatest Hits	$17.99
00138026	One Direction	$17.99
00702030	Best of Roy Orbison	$17.99
00702144	Best of Ozzy Osbourne	$14.99
00702279	Tom Petty	$17.99
00102911	Pink Floyd	$17.99
00702139	Elvis Country Favorites	$19.99
00702293	The Very Best of Prince	$19.99
00699415	Best of Queen for Guitar	$16.99
00109279	Best of R.E.M.	$14.99
00702208	Red Hot Chili Peppers — Greatest Hits	$17.99
00198960	The Rolling Stones	$17.99
00174793	The Very Best of Santana	$16.99
00702196	Best of Bob Seger	$16.99
00146046	Ed Sheeran	$17.99

00702252	Frank Sinatra — Nothing But the Best	$12.99
00702010	Best of Rod Stewart	$17.99
00702049	Best of George Strait	$17.99
00702259	Taylor Swift for Easy Guitar	$15.99
00359800	Taylor Swift – Easy Guitar Anthology	$24.99
00702260	Taylor Swift — Fearless	$14.99
00139727	Taylor Swift — 1989	$19.99
00115960	Taylor Swift — Red	$16.99
00253667	Taylor Swift — Reputation	$17.99
00702290	Taylor Swift — Speak Now	$16.99
00232849	Chris Tomlin Collection – 2nd Edition	$14.99
00702226	Chris Tomlin — See the Morning	$12.95
00148643	Train	$14.99
00702427	U2 — 18 Singles	$19.99
00702108	Best of Stevie Ray Vaughan	$17.99
00279005	The Who	$14.99
00702123	Best of Hank Williams	$15.99
00194548	Best of John Williams	$14.99
00702228	Neil Young — Greatest Hits	$17.99
00119133	Neil Young — Harvest	$14.99

Prices, contents and availability subject to change without notice.

Visit Hal Leonard online at **halleonard.com**

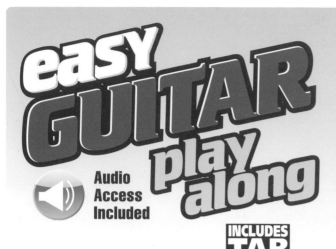

easy GUITAR play along

Audio Access Included

INCLUDES TAB

The *Easy Guitar Play Along®* series features streamlined transcriptions of your favorite songs. Just follow the tab, listen to the audio to hear how the guitar should sound, and then play along using the backing tracks. Playback tools are provided for slowing down the tempo without changing pitch and looping challenging parts. The melody and lyrics are included in the book so that you can sing or simply follow along.

1. ROCK CLASSICS

Jailbreak • Living After Midnight • Mississippi Queen • Rocks Off • Runnin' Down a Dream • Smoke on the Water • Strutter • Up Around the Bend.
00702560 Book/CD Pack....... $14.99

2. ACOUSTIC TOP HITS

About a Girl • I'm Yours • The Lazy Song • The Scientist • 21 Guns • Upside Down • What I Got • Wonderwall.
00702569 Book/CD Pack....... $14.99

3. ROCK HITS

All the Small Things • Best of You • Brain Stew (The Godzilla Remix) • Californication • Island in the Sun • Plush • Smells Like Teen Spirit • Use Somebody.
00702570 Book/CD Pack....... $14.99

4. ROCK 'N' ROLL

Blue Suede Shoes • I Get Around • I'm a Believer • Jailhouse Rock • Oh, Pretty Woman • Peggy Sue • Runaway • Wake Up Little Susie.
00702572 Book/CD Pack....... $14.99

6. CHRISTMAS SONGS

Have Yourself a Merry Little Christmas • A Holly Jolly Christmas • The Little Drummer Boy • Run Rudolph Run • Santa Claus Is Comin' to Town • Silver and Gold • Sleigh Ride • Winter Wonderland.
00101879 Book/CD Pack......... $14.99

7. BLUES SONGS FOR BEGINNERS

Come On (Part 1) • Double Trouble • Gangster of Love • I'm Ready • Let Me Love You Baby • Mary Had a Little Lamb • San-Ho-Zay • T-Bone Shuffle.
00103235 Book/
          Online Audio.......... $17.99

9. ROCK SONGS FOR BEGINNERS

Are You Gonna Be My Girl • Buddy Holly • Everybody Hurts • In Bloom • Otherside • The Rock Show • Santa Monica • When I Come Around.
00103255 Book/CD Pack..... $14.99

10. GREEN DAY

Basket Case • Boulevard of Broken Dreams • Good Riddance (Time of Your Life) • Holiday • Longview • 21 Guns • Wake Me up When September Ends • When I Come Around.
00122322 Book/
          Online Audio........ $16.99

11. NIRVANA

All Apologies • Come As You Are • Heart Shaped Box • Lake of Fire • Lithium • The Man Who Sold the World • Rape Me • Smells Like Teen Spirit.
00122325 Book/
          Online Audio........ $17.99

13. AC/DC

Back in Black • Dirty Deeds Done Dirt Cheap • For Those About to Rock (We Salute You) • Hells Bells • Highway to Hell • Rock and Roll Ain't Noise Pollution • T.N.T. • You Shook Me All Night Long.
14042895 Book/
          Online Audio........ $17.99

14. JIMI HENDRIX – SMASH HITS

All Along the Watchtower • Can You See Me • Crosstown Traffic • Fire • Foxey Lady • Hey Joe • Manic Depression • Purple Haze • Red House • Remember • Stone Free • The Wind Cries Mary.
00130591 Book/
          Online Audio........ $24.99

HAL•LEONARD®
www.halleonard.com

Prices, contents, and availability subject to change without notice.